Sensational Salads

STEP-BY-STEP

Sensational Salads

CAROLE HANDSLIP

SHOOTING STAR PRESS

This edition printed in 1995 for:
Shooting Star Press Inc
230 Fifth Avenue – Suite 1212
New York, NY 10001

Shooting Star Press books are available at special discounts for bulk purchases for sales promotions,
premiums, fund-raising, or educational use. Special edition or book excerpts can also be created to
specification. For details contact: Special Sales Director, Shooting Star Press Inc.,
230 Fifth Avenue, Suite 1212, New York, NY 10001

ISBN 1-57335-005-2

Produced by Haldane Mason, London

Printed in Italy

Acknowledgements:
Art Direction: Ron Samuels
Editor: Joanna Swinnerton
Series Design: Pedro & Frances Prá-Lopez/Kingfisher Design
Page Design: Somewhere Creative
Photography: Iain Bagwell
Stylist: Rachel Jukes
Home Economist: Carole Handslip

Photographs on pages 6, 20, 34, 48 & 64 are reproduced by permission of
ZEFA Picture Library (UK) Ltd.

Note:
*Unless otherwise stated, milk is assumed to be full-fat, eggs are AA large and pepper is freshly
ground black pepper.*

Contents

✻

CHAPTER ONE

Appetizer Salads

✤

The first course of any meal should be tantalizing to the taste buds and not too heavy, so salads fit the bill perfectly. They provide an infinite variety of taste, texture, and color, and a superb opportunity for the cook to display an imaginative flair and get the meal off to a good start by pleasing the eye as well as the appetite.

Use pretty dishes to complement your chosen salad: scallop shells for example, or other interesting shapes; or perhaps glass plates, which can be plain, colored, decorated, or frosted. Take care over the decoration and garnish, and use sprigs of fresh herbs where possible. Serve a first course salad with Melba toast or with one of the many exciting Mediterranean breads available, which are flavored with oils and aromatic herbs. These are particularly suitable, as they can be served warm, in satisfying chunks, attractively arranged in a basket.

Opposite: Use the freshest vegetables in contrasting colors for a striking effect. Vivid reds and greens are particularly effective.

STEP 1

STEP 2

STEP 3

STEP 4

ARTICHOKE & PROSCIUTTO SALAD

A pretty salad with a piquant flavor. Use bottled artichokes rather than canned ones if possible, as they have a better flavor. Basil has a warm, pungent aroma that blends particularly well with tomato.

SERVES 4

9-ounce bottle artichokes in oil, drained
4 small tomatoes
$^1/_4$ cup sun-dried tomatoes, cut into strips
$^1/_4$ cup black olives, halved and pitted
$^1/_4$ cup prosciutto, cut into strips
1 tbsp chopped fresh basil

FRENCH DRESSING:
3 tbsp olive oil
1 tbsp wine vinegar
1 small garlic clove, crushed
$^1/_2$ tsp Dijon or Meaux mustard
1 tsp clear honey
salt and pepper

1 Drain the artichokes thoroughly, then cut them into quarters, and place in a bowl.

2 Cut each tomato into 6 wedges, and place in the bowl with the sun-dried tomatoes, olives, and prosciutto.

3 To make the dressing, put all the ingredients into a screw-top jar and shake vigorously until the ingredients are thoroughly blended.

4 Pour the dressing over the salad, and toss well together.

5 Transfer to individual plates, and sprinkle with the basil.

P R O S C I U T T O

This Italian ham is first dry-cured, and then matured for about a year. Once it is dried, it can then be sliced very thinly and is served raw. It can be found in most supermarkets and in Italian delis.

STEP 1

STEP 2

STEP 3

STEP 4

SEAFOOD WITH TOMATO VINAIGRETTE

Packages of frozen mixed seafood are now available, which makes this spectacular salad very quick and easy to assemble.

SERVES 4–6

1 red bell pepper
2 tomatoes
12-ounce package mixed seafood, defrosted
    and well drained
few sprigs of dill
lemon slices, to garnish

TOMATO VINAIGRETTE:
2 tomatoes, skinned and finely chopped
2 tsp tomato paste
4 tbsp olive oil
1 tsp wine vinegar
1 garlic clove, crushed
salt and pepper

1 Cut the red bell pepper in half, and remove the seeds. Lay the red bell pepper halves cut-side down on a broiler pan, and cook slowly under a preheated medium broiler until blackened.

2 Put the bell pepper into a plastic bag to cool, then remove the skin, and chop the flesh roughly.

3 Cut each tomato into 8 wedges, and place in a bowl with the bell pepper and drained seafood.

4 To make the vinaigrette, put all the ingredients in a bowl, and whisk together.

5 Pour the vinaigrette over the seafood, and mix thoroughly.

6 Arrange the seafood salad on individual plates. Sprinkle with dill sprigs, and garnish with lemon slices. Serve with Tomato Toasts (see page 12).

SEAFOOD

If you cannot find frozen mixed seafood, buy the fish individually from the fresh fish counter. Use a mixture of shrimp, raw squid prepared and cut into thin rings, and mussels. The mussels should be cleaned and cooked for 4 minutes before being removed from their shells. A few poached scallops cut into pieces would make a really special addition.

STEP 1

STEP 2

STEP 3

STEP 4

MEDITERRANEAN BELL PEPPER SALAD

Colorful bell peppers fried with zucchini and onion are marinated in balsamic vinegar and anchovies to make a tasty appetizer. Serve with fresh bread or Tomato Toasts (shown on page 11).

SERVES 4

1 onion
2 red bell peppers
2 yellow bell peppers
3 tbsp olive oil
2 large zucchini, sliced
2 garlic cloves, sliced
1 tbsp balsamic vinegar
8 chopped anchovy fillets
$^1/_4$ cup black olives, halved and pitted
1 tbsp chopped fresh basil
salt and pepper

TOMATO TOASTS:
small stick of French bread
1 garlic clove, crushed
1 tomato, skinned and chopped
2 tbsp olive oil
salt and pepper

1 Cut the onion into wedges. Core and deseed the bell peppers, and cut into thick slices.

2 Heat the oil in a large heavy-bottomed skillet. Add the onion, bell peppers, zucchini, and garlic, and fry slowly for 20 minutes, stirring occasionally.

3 Add the vinegar, anchovies, olives, and seasoning to taste. Mix thoroughly, and let cool.

4 Spoon onto individual plates, and sprinkle with the basil.

5 To make the Tomato Toasts, cut the French bread diagonally into $^1/_2$-in. slices.

6 Mix the garlic, tomato and seasoning together, and spread thinly over each slice of bread.

7 Place on a cookie sheet, and drizzle with the olive oil. Bake in a preheated oven at 425°F for 5–10 minutes until crisp.

BALSAMIC VINEGAR

Balsamic vinegar is made in and around Modena in Italy. It is made from grape juice concentrated over heat and is fermented slowly in wooden barrels. It has a sweet-sour flavor, but is rich and mellow. You only need a teaspoon or two to give a dish a real zip – which is just as well, as it is quite expensive.

HEARTS OF PALM & PAPAYA SALAD

A really impressive first course, in which the colors complement each other, as do the subtly intriguing flavors. Use either the Lime & Honey or the Chervil Dressing.

STEP 1

SERVES 6

1 small papaya, halved and deseeded
1½ cups canned hearts of palm
1 bunch watercress
2 tbsp pine nuts, browned

LIME & HONEY DRESSING:
grated rind of 1 lime
3 tbsp lime juice
2 tbsp olive oil
2 tbsp clear honey
salt and pepper

CHERVIL DRESSING:
2 tbsp superfine sugar
1 tbsp boiling water
2 tbsp chopped fresh chervil
2 tbsp olive oil
3 tbsp lemon juice

1 Peel the papaya thinly and cut lengthwise into thin slices. Arrange on individual plates.

2 Drain the can of palm hearts. Cut the palm hearts diagonally into rings, and arrange over the papaya.

3 Break the watercress into sprigs, and arrange around the edge of the plates.

4 To make the Lime & Honey Dressing, mix the grated lime rind and juice with the olive oil, honey, and seasoning to taste.

5 To make the Chervil Dressing, mix the sugar, boiling water and chervil together, then mix in the olive oil and lemon juice.

6 Pour a little of the dressing over each salad, and sprinkle the pine nuts over the top.

STEP 2

STEP 3

PAPAYA

The skin of a papaya turns from green to an orangey yellow as it ripens, and should yield slightly when pressed. When you slice one in half, you will find bright salmon-pink flesh with a mass of little gray seeds. The seeds are edible, but are very hot and peppery. The flesh is delicious served simply with lime juice, but blends extremely well with other tropical fruits, or with smoked meats.

STEP 4

STEP 1

STEP 3

STEP 4

STEP 5

PEAR & ROQUEFORT SALAD

The sweetness of the pear makes it a perfect partner for radiccio, which is sharp, and arugula, which is peppery. The Roquefort dressing completes this wonderful marriage.

SERVES 4

2 ounces Roquefort cheese
²/₃ cup natural yogurt
milk (optional)
2 tbsp chopped chives
lollo rosso leaves
radiccio leaves
arugula leaves
2 ripe pears
pepper
chopped chives to garnish

1 Mash the cheese with a fork, and blend in the yogurt gradually until smooth, adding a little milk if necessary. Add the chives with pepper to taste.

2 Break the lollo rosso leaves into manageable pieces. Arrange on individual plates with the radiccio and arugula leaves.

3 Quarter and core the pears, and cut into slices.

4 Arrange some pear slices over the salad on each plate.

5 Drizzle the dressing over the top, and garnish with chives.

LETTUCE

If you buy lettuce that is not prewashed, prepare it carefully. Break off and discard the outer leaves and any damaged leaves. Rinse the lettuce carefully and either pat dry with paper towels, or spin in a salad spinner, or wrap loosely in a dish cloth, gather up the loose ends and swing it around – simple, but effective! It is best to do this outside, as some water will leak through the cloth.

ROQUEFORT CHEESE

A blue cheese from the southern Massif Central in France, Roquefort is creamy-white with blue-green veins running through it, and has a strong flavor.

If you prefer, you can cut the Roquefort cheese into cubes, and add it to the salad greens with the pears, and pour a herb vinaigrette, such as the Chervil Dressing on page 15, over the salad.

STEP 1

STEP 3

STEP 3

STEP 4

SMOKED TROUT & APPLE SALAD

Smoked trout and horseradish are natural partners, but with apple and watercress this makes a wonderful first course. I like to serve this dish with Melba toast.

SERVES 4

2 orange-red eating apples, quartered and
   cored
2 tbsp French Dressing (see page 8)
¹/₂ bunch watercress
1 smoked trout, skinned and boned, about
   6 ounces

HORSERADISH DRESSING:
¹/₂ cup natural yogurt
¹/₂–1 tsp lemon juice
1 tbsp horseradish sauce
milk (optional)
salt and pepper

TO GARNISH:
1 tbsp chopped chives
chive flowers (optional)

1 Slice the apples into a bowl, and toss in the French dressing to prevent them from browning.

2 Break the watercress into sprigs, and arrange on 4 serving plates.

3 Flake the trout into fairly large pieces, and arrange between the watercress with the apple.

4 To make the horseradish dressing, whisk all the ingredients together, adding a little milk if too thick. Drizzle over the trout. Sprinkle over the chives and flowers if you have them.

CHIVE FLOWERS

Chives produce very attractive purple flowers in early summer, and these are excellent to use as a garnish both for their appearance and flavor. Each floret should be pulled gently from the round flower head and sprinkled over the salad.

MELBA TOAST

To make Melba toast, toast thinly sliced bread, then cut off the crusts and carefully slice in half horizontally, using a sharp knife. Cut in half diagonally, and place in a warm oven for 15–20 minutes until the edges start to curl and the toast is crisp.

CHAPTER TWO

Leafy Salads

❀

Corn salad, arugula, purslane, chicory, endive, escarole, and radiccio are just a few of the many interesting and delicious salad leaves available – eaten either on their own or in combination, they help to make a very interesting and attractive salad. Add a few herbs and a simple dressing using extra virgin olive oil and a mellow vinegar such as balsamic or sherry vinegar and you have the most simple, yet delicious salad accompaniment.

Flowers add flavor and color to green salads; many flowers are edible, and herb flowers such as chives, thyme, or marjoram are full of flavor. Nasturtiums, primroses, violas, and geraniums are all easily obtainable at different times of the year and look stunning sprinkled over the top of salad leaves.

Opposite: *An enormous range of lettuces, salad greens and fresh herbs is available, and can make even a simple salad look exotic and smell deliciously aromatic.*

STEP 3

STEP 4

STEP 5

STEP 7

CAESAR SALAD

This salad is traditionally made with romaine lettuce, although any crisp variety can be used.

SERVES 4

4 tbsp olive oil
2 tbsp lemon juice
2 garlic cloves, crushed
1 tsp Worcestershire sauce
1 egg
6 quail's eggs
1 large romaine lettuce
1-ounce block of Parmesan cheese
2 slices bread, crusts removed
4 tbsp corn oil
salt and pepper

1 Mix together the olive oil, lemon juice, garlic, and Worcestershire sauce with salt and pepper to taste. Put the single egg in a blender or food processor, and blend for 30 seconds. Add the oil mixture gradually through the feeder tube until the dressing thickens slightly.

2 If you do not have a food processor, you can make the dressing using a hand-held electric mixer, or a hand whisk. Put the egg into a small bowl, and whisk in the garlic, Worcestershire sauce, and seasoning. Gradually whisk in the oil, and finally add the lemon juice.

3 Boil the quail's eggs for 5 minutes, then plunge into cold water to cool. Crack the shells, and remove the eggs very carefully. Cut the eggs into quarters.

4 Tear the lettuce into manageable-sized pieces, and put into a salad bowl with the quail's eggs.

5 Using a potato peeler, shave peelings off the Parmesan cheese.

6 Cut the bread into $1/4$-in cubes, and fry in the corn oil until golden. Drain well on paper towels.

7 Pour the dressing over the salad, and toss thoroughly. Sprinkle the croûtons and Parmesan shavings over the top.

STEP 1

STEP 2

STEP 4

STEP 5

SPINACH & BACON SALAD

Use only young tender spinach leaves for this recipe, as the older ones can be rather tough.

SERVES 4

6 cups young spinach leaves
1 avocado
3 tbsp French dressing (see page 8)
2 slices bread, crusts removed
3 tbsp olive oil
5 thick slices bacon
1 garlic clove, chopped
1 tbsp cider vinegar

1 Trim the stalks from the spinach, and put the leaves into a salad bowl.

2 Halve the avocado, and remove the pit by stabbing it with a sharp knife and twisting it to loosen. Peel the avocado. Slice into a small bowl, and toss in the French dressing until well coated. Add to the spinach, and toss together.

3 Cut the bread into small triangles, and fry in the olive oil until golden. Remove from the pan, and drain well on paper towels.

4 Cut the bacon into strips.

5 Add the bacon to the pan, and cook until it begins to brown; then add the garlic, and fry for another minute. Transfer the bacon to the salad bowl, using a perforated spoon.

6 Add the cider vinegar to the pan, and stir to dissolve any juices, then pour over the salad. Sprinkle with the croûtons.

AVOCADOS

When ripe, an avocado should yield to gentle pressure at the pointed end. If you want to ripen them quickly, place them in a fruit bowl with ripe bananas. When halved, they will turn brown very quickly, so brush the cut surfaces with lemon juice.

STEP 1

STEP 2

STEP 3

STEP 4

MIXED LEAF SALAD WITH FLOWERS

A green leafy salad made from as many varieties of salad leaves and flowers as you can find.

SERVES 6

½ head chicory
½ head oak leaf lettuce or quattro stagione
few leaves of radiccio
1 head endive
½ cup arugula leaves
few sprigs fresh basil or flat-leaf parsley
6 tbsp French Dressing (see page 8)
flowers of your choice (see below)

1 Tear the chicory, oak leaf lettuce and radiccio into manageable pieces.

2 Place the salad greens into a large serving bowl, or individual bowls if you prefer.

3 Cut the endive into diagonal slices, and add to the bowl with the arugula leaves, and basil or parsley.

4 Pour the dressing over the salad, and toss thoroughly.

5 Scatter a mixture of flowers over the top.

EDIBLE FLOWERS

Violas, rock geraniums, nasturtiums, chive flowers, and pot marigolds add vibrant colors and a sweet flavor to any salad, and will turn this simple salad into an unusual dish. Use it as a centerpiece at a dinner party, or to liven up a simple everyday meal.

ARUGULA

The young green leaves of this plant have a distinct warm, peppery flavor and are delicious used in green salads. It is extremely easy to grow, and after you have sown it in the garden or greenhouse, you will always have plenty, as it self-seeds all over the place!

ENDIVE & AVOCADO SALAD

A simple and refreshing salad to serve on hot sunny days. The contrasting colors of the pink grapefruit, creamy endive, and bright green corn salad make this a stunning accompaniment.

STEP 1

STEP 2

STEP 5

STEP 6

SERVES 4

1 pink grapefruit
1 avocado
1 package corn salad, washed thoroughly
2 heads endive, sliced diagonally
1 tbsp chopped fresh mint

FRENCH DRESSING:
3 tbsp olive oil
1 tbsp wine vinegar
1 small garlic clove, crushed
$\frac{1}{2}$ tsp Dijon or Meaux mustard
1 tsp clear honey
salt and pepper

1 Peel the grapefruit with a serrated knife.

2 Cut the grapefruit into segments by cutting between the membranes.

3 To make the French dressing, put all the ingredients into a screw-top jar, and shake vigorously.

4 Halve the avocado, and remove the pit by stabbing the pit with a sharp knife and twisting to loosen. Remove the skin.

5 Cut the avocado into small slices, put into a bowl and toss in the French dressing.

6 Remove any stalks from the corn salad and put into a bowl with the grapefruit, endive and mint.

7 Add the avocado and 2 tablespoons of the French dressing. Toss well, and transfer to serving plates.

CORN SALAD

This is also called lamb's lettuce because the shape of its dark green leaves resembles a lamb's tongue. The French call it **mâche**. It is easy to grow in the garden and will withstand the frost.

STEP 2

STEP 4

STEP 5

STEP 6

ARUGULA & ORANGE SALAD WITH LEMON DRESSING

Pine nuts give a delicious flavor to this salad, but be careful when browning them, as they burn very easily.

SERVES 4

1 head of chicory
2 oranges
1 avocado, halved and pitted
$\frac{1}{4}$ cup pine nuts
$\frac{1}{2}$ cup arugula leaves

LEMON DRESSING:
finely grated rind of $\frac{1}{2}$ lemon
2 tbsp lemon juice
2 tbsp olive oil
1 tsp clear honey
salt and pepper

1 Tear the chicory into manageable pieces, and place in a salad bowl.

2 Remove the pith and rind from the oranges, and cut the flesh into segments. Put the flesh into the salad bowl.

3 Peel the avocado, and cut into slices. Put the slices into the salad bowl.

4 Heat a heavy-bottomed skillet. Add the pine nuts and cook until they are golden, shaking the pan constantly.

5 Whisk all the dressing ingredients together with seasoning to taste.

6 Add the arugula leaves to the salad bowl. Pour over the dressing, and toss thoroughly.

PITTING AN AVOCADO

To pit an avocado, cut through to the pit lengthwise, then twist the two halves against each other to separate. Chop into the pit with a sharp knife so that it sticks in firmly, then twist sharply. This will release the pit, which will come away with the knife.

STEP 1

STEP 2

STEP 3

STEP 4

CHICORY SALAD WITH NASTURTIUMS

The addition of nasturtiums make this unusual salad very appealing to the eye, and will be a talking point at any dinner party.

SERVES 4

½ head chicory
8-ounce package corn salad, washed
*   thoroughly*
2 slices bread, crusts removed
4 tbsp corn oil for frying
nasturtium flowers

FRENCH DRESSING:
3 tbsp olive oil
1 tbsp wine vinegar
1 small garlic clove, crushed
½ tsp Dijon or Meaux mustard
1 tsp clear honey
salt and pepper

1 Tear the chicory into manageable pieces, and put into a bowl.

2 Trim the roots of the corn salad and add to the bowl.

3 Cut the bread into ½-in. cubes. Heat the corn oil in a skillet.

4 Fry the cubes of bread until golden-brown. Remove from the pan, and drain well on paper towels

5 To make the French dressing, put all the ingredients in a screw-top jar, and shake vigorously until blended. Pour 4 tablespoons of dressing over the salad, and toss thoroughly.

6 Sprinkle the croûtons over the salad, and arrange the nasturtium flowers on top.

TIPS

It is easier to cut bread into neat cubes if it is half-frozen. You can use either white or brown bread for croûtons.

For a slightly different dressing, add 1 tablespoon of chopped herbs such as chives and mint.

Nasturtium flowers have a peppery bite that enhances the flavor of any green salad. Nasturtiums are well worth cultivating both for the leaves and flowers, and they are now available in many supermarkets.

CHAPTER THREE

Main Course Salads

❦

There are plenty of ideas here for quick, colorful, delicious lunches, perfect for a summer's day. Some of the recipes will give you the chance to try a warm salad, such as Warm Calf's Liver Salad and Turkish Lamb Salad, which have enticing hot dressings poured over them just before they are served. Most can be prepared in advance, so you merely do an assembly job when you are ready to eat, allowing you to spend more time in the sun than in the kitchen.

Included here are the traditional Greek Salad, *Horiatiki*, made with tomatoes, Feta cheese, and olives; and Salad Niçoise from Provence – wonderful served with your favorite wine in the shade of a leafy tree.

A basketful of Italian bread, some olive bread, an onion baguette or some Tomato Toasts (page 12) will enhance any of these salads enormously.

Opposite: Main course salads can be made of almost anything, from the traditional salad ingredients to fruit, winter vegetables, cheese, meat, nuts, beans, and lentils.

STEP 1

STEP 2

STEP 4

STEP 4

GREEK SALAD

A rustic, peasant salad that makes a delicious lunch on a hot sunny day. Remember that Feta cheese is inclined to be salty, so go lightly with seasoning.

SERVES 4

¹/₂ *English cucumber*
1 small onion, sliced thinly into rings
1 green bell pepper, cored, deseeded and chopped
1 pound tomatoes
4 tbsp olive oil
1 tbsp cider vinegar
1 tbsp chopped fresh basil
1 tbsp chopped fresh oregano
8 ounces Feta cheese
salt and pepper
¹/₂ *cup black olives, pitted, to garnish*

1 Cut the cucumber into large dice, and put into a bowl with the sliced onion and chopped green bell pepper.

2 Cut each tomato into 8 wedges, and add to the bowl with the oil, vinegar, herbs, and salt and pepper to taste.

3 Toss all the ingredients thoroughly, and transfer to a salad bowl.

4 Cut the Feta cheese into cubes. Sprinkle the cheese evenly over the salad.

5 Garnish with the olives, and serve with plenty of crusty bread to mop up the juices.

TIP

Use Greek kalamata olives if possible. They are a purple-brown color and have a superior flavor to other varieties.

FETA CHEESE

Feta cheese is a Greek cheese traditionally made from ewe's milk and preserved in brine. Now it is often made from cow's milk. It is a white crumbly cheese with a firm texture, and is often quite salty, depending on how long it has been left in brine.

STEP 1

STEP 2

STEP 3

STEP 4

CHICKEN & GRAPES IN CURRY MAYONNAISE

Tender chicken breast, sweet grapes and crisp celery coated in a mild curry mayonnaise make a wonderful al fresco lunch served with spiced rice and a green salad.

SERVES 4

1 pound cooked chicken breast
2 celery stalks
2 cups black grapes
$^1/_2$ cup split almonds, browned
paprika
fresh cilantro or flat-leaf parsley to
  garnish

CURRY MAYONNAISE:
$^2/_3$ cup mayonnaise
$^1/_2$ cup natural fromage frais
1 tbsp clear honey
1 tbsp curry sauce

1 Cut the chicken into fairly large pieces, and slice the celery finely.

2 Halve the grapes, and remove the seeds. Place in a bowl with the chicken and celery.

3 To make the curry mayonnaise, mix all the ingredients together until blended.

4 Pour the mayonnaise over the salad, and mix together carefully until well coated.

5 Transfer to a shallow serving dish, and sprinkle with the almonds and paprika. Garnish with the cilantro or parsley.

BROWNING ALMONDS

To brown almonds, place on a cookie sheet in a medium-hot oven for 5–10 minutes until golden-brown. Alternatively, they can be browned under a medium broiler, turning frequently, as they burn quickly. Cool before adding to the salad so that they are crisp.

CILANTRO

Cilantro is an intensely aromatic herb which is used extensively in Mexican and Indian cookery. The seeds (coriander) are ground to give a warm spicy flavor quite unlike that of fresh cilantro. Its pretty lacy leaves make it an excellent, attractive garnish.

STEP 2

STEP 3

STEP 4

STEP 5

PASTA PROVENCAL

Use any pasta shape for this salad, but drain the pasta thoroughly so that it does not dilute the dressing. You could substitute tuna fish for the chicken to make a change.

SERVES 4

6 ounces dried pasta shapes
4 tbsp French Dressing (see page 8)
12 ounces chicken breast
2 tbsp olive oil
2 zucchini
1 red bell pepper
2 garlic cloves
4 tomatoes
2-ounce can of anchovies, drained
1/4 cup black olives
sprig of fresh parsley to garnish

1 Cook the pasta in boiling salted water for 10–12 minutes until *al dente*. Drain and rinse in hot water, then drain again thoroughly.

2 Put into a bowl with the dressing, and mix together.

3 Cut the chicken breast into strips. Heat the oil in a skillet. Add the chicken, and stir-fry for 4–5 minutes, stirring occasionally until cooked, then remove from the pan.

4 Slice the zucchini. Core and deseed the red bell pepper, and cut into chunks. Slice the garlic, and add to the pan with the zucchini and bell pepper.

Fry for 12–15 minutes, stirring occasionally, until softened.

5 Cut the tomatoes into wedges. Chop the anchovies roughly. Halve and pit the olives. Add to the pasta with the chicken and fried vegetables, and mix together.

6 Transfer to a serving dish. Garnish with parsley, and serve immediately while warm.

PASTA SHAPES

For some suitable pasta shapes, choose from the following; farfalle (bow ties), conchiglie (shells), conchiglie rigate (ridged shells), penne (quill shapes), rigatoni (tubular pasta, usually ridged), fusilli (spiral shapes), rotelle (wheels), and orecchiette (little ears).

TURKISH LAMB SALAD

The bread in this salad is an unusual addition, but it soaks up the dressing well and has a delicious flavor. The charred meat and creamy yogurt complete a delightful salad for a light lunch.

STEP 2

STEP 3

STEP 4

STEP 5

SERVES 4

2 red bell peppers, cored and deseeded
1 yellow bell pepper, cored and deseeded
1 green bell pepper, cored and deseeded
4 tomatoes, skinned
1 small onion
1 pound lamb tenderloin
3 pitta breads
4 tbsp Tomato Vinaigrette (see page 10)
$1/2$ cup thick, creamy yogurt
3 tbsp chopped fresh parsley

1 To skin the bell peppers, lay them cut-side down on a broiler pan, and cook slowly until blackened. Put in a plastic bag to cool.

2 Remove the bell pepper skin, and chop the flesh roughly. Cut each tomato into 8 wedges. Slice the onion. Put the onion into a bowl with the tomato wedges and bell pepper chunks.

3 Place the lamb tenderloin under a preheated medium-hot broiler until charred on the outside but still pink in the middle.

4 Cut the bread into pieces, and add to the bowl with the bell peppers, onion and tomato. Pour over the dressing. Mix together thoroughly, and arrange on individual plates.

5 Slice the lamb, and arrange a few pieces over each salad. Drizzle the yogurt over the top, and sprinkle with the parsley.

VARIATION

You may prefer to use a half leg of lamb instead of lamb tenderloin. If so, cut it into cubes, and thread the meat onto skewers. Cook for 3–4 minutes on each side under a hot broiler. Then slide off the skewers, and arrange over the salad.

STEP 2

STEP 4

STEP 5

STEP 6

WARM CALF'S LIVER SALAD

The delicate flavor of calf's liver is enhanced with a dressing of balsamic vinegar and fresh sage. The liver should be cooked very briefly so that it is still pink inside. Chicken livers can be used instead of calf's liver, if you prefer.

SERVES 2

8-ounce package of mixed salad greens
8 ounces calf's liver
1 orange, cut into segments
2 tbsp pine nuts
3 tbsp olive oil
1 garlic clove, sliced
2 tsp chopped sage
2 tbsp balsamic vinegar
salt and pepper

1 Arrange the salad greens on 2 individual plates. Cut the liver into large pieces.

2 Peel the orange using a serrated knife, then divide into segments.

3 Put the pine nuts in a small heavy-bottomed skillet and cook over a medium heat, shaking the pan constantly so that the nuts do not burn.

4 Heat the oil in a heavy-bottomed skillet. Add the liver to the pan with the garlic and sage, and fry for 1–2 minutes, depending on the thickness of the liver, turning it once.

5 Remove the liver from the skillet, using a perforated spoon, and arrange on the salad with the orange segments.

6 Add the vinegar to the skillet with any juices from the orange, and stir well to deglaze the pan. Season to taste.

7 Sprinkle the pine nuts over the salads, then pour over the juices and serve immediately.

CALF'S LIVER

Calf's liver is generally considered to be the finest in quality and flavor, but is also the most expensive. It should be thinly sliced and fried briefly, so that it is still pink inside.

STEP 2

STEP 3

STEP 4

STEP 6

SALADE NICOISE

An ideal salad for a summer lunch. It is particularly delicious served with hot garlic bread.

SERVES 4

1 small crisp lettuce
1 pound tomatoes
7-ounce can of tuna fish, drained
2 tbsp chopped fresh parsley
1/2 English cucumber
1 small red onion, sliced
1 1/2 cups green beans, ends trimmed, cooked
1 small red bell pepper, cored and deseeded
6 tbsp French Dressing (see page 8)
3 hard-cooked eggs
2-ounce can of anchovies, drained
12 black olives, pitted

1 Place the lettuce leaves in a mixing bowl.

2 Cut the tomatoes into wedges, and flake the tuna fish. Put both into the bowl with the parsley.

3 Cut the cucumber in half lengthwise, then cut into slices. Slice the onion. Add the cucumber and onion to the bowl.

4 Cut the green beans in half. Chop the red bell pepper. Add the beans and bell pepper to the bowl.

5 Pour over the French dressing, and toss thoroughly, then spoon into a salad bowl to serve.

6 Cut the eggs into quarters, and arrange over the top with the anchovies. Scatter with the olives.

GARLIC BREAD

To make garlic bread, cream 1/3 cup butter with 2 crushed garlic cloves and seasoning to taste. Slice a French stick diagonally without cutting right through, so the pieces stay attached. Spread both sides of each slice with the garlic butter. Wrap in foil, and put in a hot oven for about 10 minutes. Unwrap and leave in the oven to crisp for 5 minutes.

CHAPTER FOUR

Substantial Salads

❧

Many of these salads are delicious served warm and can be prepared quickly just before you eat. Comforting warm lentils with frankfurters are enlivened with a tomato and olive dressing. Warm pasta tossed in a fresh basil vinaigrette tastes wonderful. Beans too make a delicious salad, as many varieties as you like – the more the merrier when it comes to a mixture of colors and flavors. Enhance them with a dressing of soy sauce and garlic, and for that extra zip, add a bouquet of chopped cilantro.

There are salads here to satisfy every taste and appetite, from the gourmet to the ravenous, from the delicate flavor of wild rice with mint and mango to a hugely satisfying hot potato salad in a garlicky dressing of olives and tomato.

Opposite: The addition of filling ingredients such as potatoes and root vegetables to the usual range of salad ingredients turns any salad into a satisfying meal.

STEP 2

STEP 3

STEP 4

STEP 5

WARM PASTA WITH BASIL VINAIGRETTE

All the ingredients of pesto sauce are included here – basil, pine nuts, Parmesan cheese, and olive oil. Sun-dried tomatoes and olives complete this delicious salad, which is just as tasty served cold.

SERVES 4

2 cups dried pasta spirals
4 tomatoes
½ cup black olives
¼ cup sun-dried tomatoes
2 tbsp pine nuts, browned (see page 30)
2 tbsp Parmesan cheese shavings
sprig of fresh basil to garnish

BASIL VINAIGRETTE:
4 tbsp chopped fresh basil
1 garlic clove, crushed
2 tbsp grated Parmesan cheese
4 tbsp olive oil
2 tbsp lemon juice
pepper

1 Cook the pasta in boiling salted water for 10–12 minutes until *al dente*. Drain and rinse well in hot water, then drain again thoroughly.

2 To make the vinaigrette, mix the basil, garlic, Parmesan cheese, olive oil, lemon juice, and pepper together with a whisk until blended.

3 Put the pasta into a bowl, and pour over the basil vinaigrette. Toss thoroughly.

4 Skin the tomatoes, and cut into wedges. Halve and pit the olives. Slice the sun-dried tomatoes.

5 Add them all to the pasta, and mix together thoroughly. Transfer to a salad bowl, and scatter the pine nuts and Parmesan shavings over the top. Serve warm, garnished with a sprig of basil.

SUN-DRIED TOMATOES

Sun-dried tomatoes are, as their name indicates, tomatoes that have been halved and dried in the sun, leaving a wrinkled specimen with an extremely rich, concentrated flavor. They are usually immersed in oil, and herbs and garlic are added to give extra flavor. When added to a sauce or salad, they impart an added depth of flavor, and are also delicious eaten straight from the jar with a chunk of fresh bread.

STEP 1

STEP 2

STEP 3

STEP 5

LENTIL & FRANKFURTER SALAD

The tiny brown-green lentils are the finest – they have a really distinctive flavor. The larger green or brown lentils are also good and ideal in salads, as they retain their shape when cooked.

SERVES 8

1 cup green lentils
4 tbsp sunflower oil
1 tbsp soy sauce
1 tbsp wine vinegar
1 garlic clove, crushed
4 frankfurters
1 onion
1 red bell pepper
2 celery stalks
4 tomatoes
2 tbsp chopped fresh parsley
1 tbsp chopped fresh marjoram
salt and pepper

1 Put the lentils into a pan of boiling salted water. Bring back to a boil, and cook for 35–40 minutes until softened. Drain well, and put into a bowl.

2 Add the oil, soy sauce, vinegar, and garlic with seasoning to taste, and mix with the lentils while still warm. Let cool.

3 Cut the frankfurters into diagonal slices. Chop the onion finely.

4 Core and deseed the bell pepper, and chop roughly.

5 Cut the celery into thin diagonal slices.

6 Skin the tomatoes, and cut into slices. Add to the lentils with the frankfurters, onion, bell pepper, celery and herbs. Mix together well, and transfer to a serving dish.

VARIATION

Instead of frankfurters, you could use cubes of smoked ham or chopped fried bacon.

STEP 2

STEP 3

STEP 4

STEP 5

MANGO & WILD RICE SALAD

Technically, wild rice is not rice at all but comes from a wild aquatic grass native to North America. It has a nutty flavor, and is slightly chewy. Add the dressing while the rice is still hot; this way it absorbs the flavor better.

SERVES 4

$^1/_3$ cup wild rice
$^1/_3$ cup basmati rice
3 tbsp hazelnut oil
1 tbsp sherry vinegar
1 small mango
2 celery stalks
$^1/_2$ cup chopped ready-to-eat dried apricots
$^1/_2$ cup split almonds, browned
2 tbsp chopped fresh mint
salt and pepper

1 Cook the rice in separate saucepans in boiling salted water – the wild rice for 45–50 minutes, the basmati for 10–12 minutes. Drain, rinse well, and drain again thoroughly.

2 Mix the oil, vinegar, and seasoning together, and pour over the rice in a salad bowl.

3 Cut the mango in half lengthwise as close to the pit as possible. Remove the pit, using a sharp knife.

4 Peel off the skin, and cut the flesh into slices.

5 Slice the celery finely, and add to the cooled rice with the apricots,

mango, browned almonds, and chopped mint. Mix together thoroughly and transfer to a serving bowl.

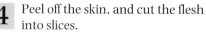

BROWNING ALMONDS

To brown almonds, place on a cookie sheet in a medium-hot oven for 5–10 minutes until golden-brown. Alternatively, they can be browned under a medium broiler, turning frequently, as they burn quickly. Cool before adding to the salad so that they are crisp.

POTATOES IN TOMATO & OLIVE DRESSING

The warm potatoes quickly absorb the wonderful flavors of olives, tomatoes and olive oil. I love this salad when served warm, but it is also good served cold.

STEP 2

STEP 3

STEP 4

STEP 5

SERVES 4

1½ pounds waxy potatoes
1 shallot
2 tomatoes
1 tbsp chopped fresh basil
salt

TOMATO AND OLIVE DRESSING:
1 tomato, skinned and chopped finely
4 black olives, pitted and chopped finely
4 tbsp olive oil
1 tbsp wine vinegar
1 garlic clove, crushed
salt and pepper

1 Cook the potatoes in boiling salted water for 15 minutes until they are tender.

2 Drain the potatoes well. Chop roughly, and put into a bowl.

3 Chop the shallot. Cut the tomatoes into wedges. Add the shallot and tomatoes to the potatoes.

4 To make the dressing, put all the ingredients into a screw-top jar, and shake vigorously.

5 Pour the dressing over the potato mixture, and toss thoroughly.

6 Transfer the salad to a serving dish and sprinkle with the chopped fresh basil.

TIPS

I often make this with mealy potatoes. It doesn't look so attractive, as the potatoes break up when they are cooked, but they absorb the dressing wonderfully.

Be sure to use an extra virgin olive oil for the dressing to give a really fruity flavor to the potatoes.

STEP 1

STEP 2

STEP 4

STEP 5

BEAN SALAD WITH SOY DRESSING

Any canned beans can be used in this salad; there are a wide variety available. To make a light lunch, I add a spicy garlic sausage or some flaked tuna fish.

SERVES 8

1½ cups canned small navy beans, drained
1½ cups canned red kidney beans, drained
1½ cups canned pinto beans, drained
½ red onion, finely sliced
1 cup green beans, ends trimmed
1 red bell pepper
2 tbsp chopped fresh cilantro
sprig of fresh cilantro to garnish

SOY DRESSING:
½-in. piece gingerroot
1 garlic clove
3 tbsp olive oil
2 tsp red wine vinegar
½ tbsp soy sauce
1 tsp chili sauce
1 tsp sesame oil

1 Put the small navy, red kidney, and pinto beans into a bowl. Add the sliced onion to the beans.

2 Cut the green beans into 1-in lengths, and cook in boiling salted water for 10 minutes until just tender. Drain thoroughly, and add to the bowl.

3 Lay the red bell pepper cut-side down on a broiler pan, and broil slowly until blackened. Put in a plastic

bag to cool. Remove the skin, and chop roughly.

4 To make the dressing, chop the gingerroot finely. Crush the garlic, and place in a screw-top jar with the olive oil, vinegar, soy sauce, chili sauce, and sesame oil. Shake vigorously.

5 Add the dressing to the salad with the red bell pepper and cilantro, and mix together thoroughly. Transfer to a serving dish, and garnish with a sprig of cilantro.

VARIATION

For a change, you could use garbanzo beans instead of one of the kinds of bean listed here. Frozen fava beans or peas also make pleasant alternatives.

STEP 1

STEP 2

STEP 4

STEP 5

WARM BULGAR & CILANTRO SALAD

Bulgar is cracked wheat, partially cooked. It is ready to eat after soaking, and needs no more cooking. Cilantro has a pungent smell that you either love or hate. It gives this salad an exciting bite.

SERVES 4

1½ cups bulgar wheat
1 onion
1 garlic clove
1 red bell pepper
3 tbsp olive oil
2 tsp ground cumin
2 tsp ground coriander
2 tomatoes
2 tbsp lemon juice
4 tbsp currants
2 tbsp chopped fresh cilantro
4 tbsp pine nuts, browned

1 Pour boiling, salted water over the bulgar wheat, and leave to soak for 20 minutes. Chop the onion and garlic. Core, deseed and chop the red bell pepper.

2 Heat the oil in a pan, and fry the onion, garlic and bell pepper for about 5 minutes until softened.

3 Add the spices, and cook for an additional 1 minute.

4 Drain the bulgar through a strainer, pressing out as much liquid as possible.

5 Chop the tomatoes. Add to the pan with the bulgar, lemon juice, and currants, and mix together thoroughly.

6 Transfer to a serving dish. Sprinkle with the cilantro and pine nuts. Serve while warm.

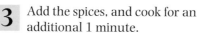

HELPFUL HINTS

Cous-cous can be used instead of bulgar wheat for this salad, and is prepared in a similar manner. Cous-cous is semolina grains that have been dampened and rolled in flour.

STEP 2

STEP 4

STEP 5

STEP 6

POTATO & SMOKED HAM IN MUSTARD MAYONNAISE

A delicious mixture of potato, egg and smoked ham mixed with a mustard mayonnaise, ideal for a light lunch. You can use sliced frankfurters cut into cubes instead of the smoked ham if you prefer.

SERVES 4

1½ pounds new potatoes, scrubbed
4 scallions, chopped
2 tbsp French Dressing (see page 8)
⅔ cup mayonnaise
3 tbsp thick natural yogurt
1 tbsp Dijon mustard
2 eggs
8-ounce slice of smoked ham
3 dill pickles
2 tbsp chopped fresh dill

1 Cook the potatoes in boiling salted water for 15 minutes until just tender, then drain.

2 Cut the potatoes into pieces, and while still warm, put into a bowl with the scallion and dressing. Mix together.

3 Mix the mayonnaise, yogurt and mustard together.

4 Boil the eggs for 12 minutes, then plunge into cold water to cool. Shell and chop roughly.

5 Cut the smoked ham into cubes. Slice the dill pickles.

6 Add to the potatoes with the egg. Pour over the mayonnaise, and mix together thoroughly, but carefully.

7 Transfer to a serving dish, and sprinkle with the dill.

DILL

Dill is a very popular herb in Scandinavia, central Europe and Russia. It is particularly good with cucumber, beet, fish and potato dishes. It has very pretty delicate, feathery fronds which makes it an excellent garnish too. Fennel would be a good substitute, but has a stronger, more aniseedy flavor.

CHAPTER FIVE

Fruit Salads

✻

Italy, Scandinavia, and the Caribbean have all been raided to offer up their fruitful treasures. From the Caribbean there are the delights of papaya, mango, guava and my own favorite, passion-fruit. From Italy, sun-ripened figs and succulent peaches are made ever more indulgent by pouring over a liqueur-flavored cream and sugar, and then broiling them until the topping has caramelized. For the more calorie-conscious, try the Tropical Salad, a mixture of fruits from the Caribbean soaked in Jamaican rum, or Summer Fruit Salad – a mixture of soft red fruits in a sauce of orange and port wine.

If you need any addition to these exotic salads, try natural fromage frais, or a thick, creamy, natural yogurt, either as they are or with a dash of liqueur stirred in. In most of the recipes the fruits are interchangeable according to the season, so do experiment to find your favorite combination.

Opposite: *The vibrant colors of fresh fruit ensure an appealing and striking dessert.*

STEP 2

STEP 4

STEP 5

STEP 6

SUMMER FRUIT SALAD

A mixture of soft summer fruits in an orange-flavored syrup with a dash of port. Serve with fromage frais or whipped cream.

SERVES 6

¹/₃ cup superfine sugar
¹/₃ cup water
grated rind and juice of 1 small orange
2 cups redcurrants, stripped from their stalks
2 tsp arrowroot
2 tbsp port
1 cup blackberries
1 cup blueberries
³/₄ cup strawberries
1¹/₂ cups raspberries

1 Put the sugar, water and grated orange rind into a pan, and heat slowly, stirring until the sugar has dissolved.

2 Add the redcurrants and orange juice. Bring to a boil, and simmer gently for 2–3 minutes.

3 Strain the fruit, reserving the syrup, and put into a bowl.

4 Blend the arrowroot with a little water. Return the syrup to the pan. Add the arrowroot, and bring to a boil, stirring until thickened.

5 Add the port, and mix together well, then pour over the redcurrants in the bowl.

6 Add the blackberries, blueberries, strawberries and raspberries. Mix together, and let cool.

7 Serve in individual glass dishes with natural fromage frais or whipped cream.

USING FROZEN FRUIT

Although this salad is really best made with fresh fruits in season, you can achieve an acceptable result with frozen equivalents, with perhaps the exception of strawberries. The frozen fruits of the forest which you can buy in most supermarkets would be ideal.

STEP 1

STEP 2

STEP 3

STEP 5

MELON & KIWI SALAD

A refreshing fruit salad, ideal to serve after a rich meal. Charentais or cantaloupe melons are also good. Physalis (ground cherries), also known as Cape gooseberries, make a delightful decoration. Peel back the thin papery husks to expose the golden berries.

SERVES 6

$^1/_2$ Galia melon
2 kiwi fruit
1 cup green seedless grapes
1 papaya, halved
3 tbsp orange-flavored liqueur such as Cointreau
1 tbsp chopped lemon verbena, lemon balm or mint
sprigs of lemon verbena or physalis (ground cherries) to decorate

1 Remove the seeds from the melon. Cut into 4 slices, and cut away the skin. Cut the flesh into cubes, and put into a bowl.

2 Peel the kiwi fruit, and cut across into slices. Add to the melon with the grapes.

3 Remove the seeds from the papaya. Cut off the skin. Slice the flesh thickly, and cut into diagonal pieces.

4 Mix together the liqueur and lemon verbena. Pour over the fruit, and set aside for 1 hour, stirring it occasionally.

5 Spoon into glasses, and pour over the juices. Decorate with lemon verbena sprigs or physalis (ground cherries).

LEMON BALM

Lemon balm or sweet balm is a fragrant lemon-scented plant with slightly hairy, serrated leaves and a pronounced lemon flavor. Lemon verbena can also be used – this has an even stronger lemon flavor and smooth elongated leaves. Both can be used as a herbal infusion, which is soothing, refreshing and delicious.

STEP 2

STEP 3

STEP 4

STEP 5

MANGO & PASSION-FRUIT SALAD WITH MASCARPONE CREAM

An exotic salad of mango, oranges and passion-fruit soaked in liqueur and served with a rich silken cream. Passion-fruit are ready to eat when their skins are well dimpled.

SERVES 4

1 large mango
2 oranges
4 passion-fruit
2 tbsp orange-flavored liqueur such as
    Grand Marnier
mint or geranium leaves to decorate

MASCARPONE CREAM
½ cup Mascarpone cheese
1 tbsp clear honey
4 tbsp thick, natural yogurt
few drops of vanilla extract

1 Cut the mango in half lengthwise as close to the pit as possible. Remove the pit, using a sharp knife.

2 Peel off the skin. Cut the flesh into slices, and put into a bowl.

3 Peel the oranges, removing all the pith, and cut into segments. Add to the bowl with any juices.

4 Halve the passion-fruit. Scoop out the flesh and add to the bowl with the liqueur. Mix well and chill for 1 hour. Spoon into glass dishes.

5 To make the Mascarpone cream, blend the Mascarpone cheese and honey together. Stir in the yogurt and vanilla extract until thoroughly blended.

6 Serve the fruit salad with the Mascarpone cream, decorated with mint or geranium leaves.

MASCARPONE

Mascarpone is a deliciously rich, soft cream cheese from Italy. It has a smooth silky texture with the flavor of cream. As it has a close texture, I usually add a liqueur or some yogurt to give it a softer consistency.

STEP 1

STEP 3

STEP 4

STEP 5

TROPICAL SALAD

Papayas are ready to eat when they yield to gentle pressure applied in the palm of your hand. Use baby pineapples if you can, as the salad looks even more stunning served in the shells.

SERVES 8

1 papaya
2 tbsp fresh orange juice
3 tbsp rum
2 bananas
2 guavas
1 small pineapple or 2 baby pineapples
2 passion-fruit, halved
pineapple leaves to decorate

1 Cut the papaya in half, and remove the seeds. Peel and slice the flesh into a bowl.

2 Pour over the orange juice, together with the rum.

3 Slice the bananas. Peel and slice the guavas. Add both to the bowl.

4 Cut the top and bottom from the pineapple, then cut off the skin.

5 Slice the pineapple flesh, discarding the core, and cut into pieces. Add to the bowl.

6 Halve the passion-fruit, and scoop out the flesh with a teaspoon. Add to the bowl, and stir well to mix.

7 Spoon the salad into glass bowls, and decorate with pineapple leaves.

PINEAPPLES

If you are using baby pineapples, cut them in half lengthwise and scoop out the flesh after loosening with a grapefruit knife. Cut the flesh into pieces, and use the shells to serve the salad in.

GUAVAS

Guavas come from the Caribbean, Thailand, and Central America. They have a heavenly smell when ripe – their scent will fill a whole room. They should yield to gentle pressure when ripe, and their skins should be yellow. If you cannot buy them fresh, the canned ones are very good, and have a pink tinge to the flesh.

STEP 1

STEP 2

STEP 3

STEP 4

NECTARINES IN ALMOND LIQUEUR CREAM

Nectarines, figs and strawberries are broiled with a rich liqueur-flavored cream to give a crusted sugary finish.

SERVES 4

2 nectarines or peaches
1 1/2 cups strawberries
2 figs
2/3 cup heavy cream
2 tbsp almond-flavored liqueur such as
 Amaretto di Saronno
3 tbsp brown crystal sugar

1 Halve and pit the nectarines, then slice.

2 Hull and halve the strawberries. Cut each fig into 8 wedges, and arrange on 4 flameproof plates with the strawberries and nectarines.

3 Whip the cream and liqueur together until the cream just holds its shape. Spoon over the fruit on each plate.

4 Sprinkle the sugar generously over the cream.

5 Place each plate under a preheated hot broiler until bubbling and golden. Serve immediately.

TIPS

Bananas make a good alternative if you cannot get figs. Slice them into thick, diagonal slices and toss them in lemon juice to prevent them from browning.

To make the broiling easier, you can arrange the fruit on 1 large platter, and cover it with the liqueur-flavored cream and sugar. This means that you will only have to broil once, and no one is left waiting for dessert. Everyone can then serve themselves from the central plate.

Make sure the sugar becomes a dark brown, almost burned, as this crispness adds a great texture and flavor to the fruit.

THE PERFECT SALAD

SALAD INGREDIENTS

Make sure you always use the freshest ingredients to ensure a successful salad. Try to ensure that you buy fruit and vegetables at their peak and use them within a few days of buying.

Every salad can be turned into something special with the addition of a few carefully chosen herbs to add flavor and a delicious aroma. For an extra special salad, add a few edible flowers, which look colorful and attractive, especially when mixed with a variety of salad greens.

Herbs

Herbs, which used to be so integral a part of our cookery, are now being rediscovered. Their use in any form of cooking is to be recommended, but in salads the addition of their fresh, aromatic leaves is of special value.

Do not be afraid to experiment. There are so many herbs from which to choose, such a variety of flavors, aromas, and even colors that you can ring the changes constantly.

The flowers of herbs such as thyme, rosemary, and chives can also be used to add color and flavor.

Flowers

The fascination of flowers as an attractive garnish for salads was discovered by our ancestors long ago. Apart from

SALADS

Salads are such a versatile way of eating; the variety of ingredients is so great that they can be made to suit any occasion, from the light piquant appetizer designed to stimulate the taste buds to the more substantial dish served as a main course, or the mixture of exotic fruits that makes a delicious dessert.

Salads can be fruity, fishy, meaty, eggy, cheesy, or just fresh green. All are highly nutritious, providing valuable minerals, vitamins, and the necessary fiber. They are also generally low in calories, provided you go easy on the dressing or use a fat-free dressing. It is easy to make a salad look attractive and appetizing, which will encourage your family to eat the fruits and vegetables which are so vital to their good health. It is also often a welcome dish to serve alongside richer offerings at a dinner party or celebration meal.

It is both worthwhile and interesting to take note of the various vegetables and fruits available in the stores at different seasons of the year. It is obviously best to use them when they are at their peak, and, of course, when they are in season, as they will be plentiful and cheap. A bonus for the budget!

Many unusual ingredients are now stocked by supermarkets, which can add interest to an ordinary salad. Experiment with new fruits and vegetables, buying them in small quantities to lend unusual flavors to salads made mostly from cheaper ingredients.

You will see from the recipes that I have been liberal in the use of herbs, which must be fresh. They add a unique "zip" and it can be great fun trying them out to discover which are your favorites. Experiment each time you make a salad or a dressing; try marjoram, thyme, chives, basil, mint, fennel, and dill as well as the ubiquitous parsley. Basil goes especially well with tomatoes, and fennel and dill are particularly good with cucumber, beet, and fish salads.

A salad is the ideal emergency meal. It is quick to "rustle up" and there are times when you might discover that you already have a really good combination of ingredients when you need to present a meal-in-a-moment. A rapid check of your staples might produce a can of beans or artichoke hearts. Add the couple of tomatoes and yellow bell pepper languishing in the salad drawer of the refrigerator, throw in a few sprigs of mint or basil that you have growing on the windowsill, a few olives from that jar in the corner, a splash of dressing, and you have a culinary inspiration, a super salad that you had no idea was lurking in your kitchen.

DRESSINGS

All salads depend on being well dressed, and so it is necessary to use the best ingredients. The choice of oil is particularly important.

The principal ingredients in a salad dressing are oil and vinegar with a variety of other flavorings that can be varied to suit the particular ingredients in the salad.

Salad oils

Oils are produced from various nuts, seeds and beans, and each has its own particular flavor. Unrefined oils have a superior flavor, and, although more expensive, they are definitely worth using for salad dressings.

Olive oil is the best oil for most salad dressings, as its flavor is far superior to others. Choose a green-tinged, fruity oil, which will be labeled "extra virgin" or "first pressing."

Sesame oil has a strong nutty tang, which gives an unusual flavor to dressings and is particularly good with oriental-type salads.

Sunflower and safflower oil are neutral-flavored oils and can be mixed with olive oil or used alone to produce a lighter dressing. Mayonnaise made with a combination of one of these oils and olive oil has a lighter consistency.

Walnut and hazelnut oils have the most wonderful flavor and aroma, and are usually mixed with olive oil in a French dressing. They are especially good with slightly bitter salad plants such as endive, radiccio and spinach.

Vinegars

Vinegars such as wine, cider, sherry or herb-flavored are essential for a good dressing. Malt vinegar is far too harsh, and overpowers the subtle balance of the dressing. Lemon juice may be used if you prefer, and is often preferable if the salad is fruit-based.

Cider vinegar is reputed to contain many healthy properties and valuable nutrients.

Wine vinegar is the one most commonly used for French dressing; either red or white will do.

Sherry vinegar has a rich mellow flavor which blends particularly well with walnut and hazelnut oils.

Flavored vinegars can be made from cider and wine vinegar. To do this, steep your chosen ingredient in a small bottle of vinegar for anything up to 2 weeks. Particularly good additions are basil, tarragon, garlic, thyme, mint, and rosemary. Raspberry wine vinegar can be made by adding about 12 raspberries to a bottle of vinegar.

Balsamic vinegar is dark and mellow with a sweet/sour flavor. It is expensive, but you need only a few drops or, at most, a teaspoonful to give a wonderful taste. It is made in the area around Modena in Italy, and some of it, made by traditional methods, is aged for many years in oak barrels.

Mustards

Mustards are made from black, brown or white mustard seeds, which are ground, mixed with spices, and then, usually, mixed with vinegar.

There are many flavored mustards available, including horseradish, honey, chili and tarragon.

Meaux mustard is made from mixed mustard seeds, and has a grainy texture with a warm spicy taste.

Dijon mustard, made from husked and ground mustard seeds, is a medium-hot mustard with a sharp flavor, and is the most versatile in salads. It is made in

the delightful flavor of many, the color contrast they provide is their main asset. Common sense is the best guide as to which flowers may be used whole and which should have the petals gently separated from the calyx.

It is, of course, important that the flowers should look fresh and clean, so should they need to be washed, handle with great care and pat dry with paper towels. Store them in a sealed plastic bag in the refrigerator until required. Sprinkle them over the top of the salad just before serving so that they do not become marked by the dressing.

Borage, primroses, violas, pot marigolds, nasturtiums, violets, rock geraniums, and rose petals are all suitable, and impart a sweetness and intense color contrast to any green salad. Chive flowers have a good strong flavor. They have pretty, round, mauve flower heads, which should be separated into florets before sprinkling over the salad.

SALAD DRESSINGS
Make up a large bottle of your favorite dressing and keep it in the refrigerator until required.

Sesame Dressing
A piquant dressing with a rich creamy texture. Good with beans and any oriental-type salad.

2 tbsp sesame paste (tahini)
2 tbsp cider vinegar
2 tbsp medium sherry
2 tbsp sesame oil
1 tbsp soy sauce
1 garlic clove, crushed

Put the sesame paste in a bowl and gradually mix in the vinegar and sherry until smooth. Add the remaining ingredients, and mix together thoroughly.

Tomato Dressing
A completely fat-free dressing, ideal for the calorie- and fat-conscious.

1/2 cup tomato juice
1 garlic clove, crushed
2 tbsp lemon juice
1 tbsp soy sauce
1 tsp clear honey
2 tbsp chopped chives
salt and pepper

Put all the ingredients into a screw-top jar, and shake vigorously.

Dijon, France, and only mustard made there can be labeled as such.

German mustard is a mild sweet/sour tasting mustard and is best used in Scandinavian and German salads.

SALAD GREENS
Butterhead lettuce is the one most familiar to us all. I try to avoid the hothouse variety, as the leaves are limp and floppy. There are many interesting varieties of salad greens now available, and it is worth experimenting to find your favorite. Unlike ordinary lettuce, many of these greens have a surprisingly strong and distinctive flavor.

Arugula (Roquette)
The young green leaves of this plant have a distinctive warm peppery flavor, and are delicious in green salads.

Chicory
This is a slightly bitter tasting but most attractive curly-leaved salad plant. There are two varieties: the curly chicory, which has a mop head of light-green frilly leaves, and the Batavian chicory (escarole), which has broader, smoother leaves. Before they mature, both varieties have their leaves tied together to blanch the centers, which produces light-colored tender leaves.

Chinese leaves
These are a most useful salad ingredient, with crunchy, tightly packed leaves. I like to shred them fairly finely, and use them as a base, adding bean shoots and other salad leaves such as watercress or dandelion.

Corn salad
This is also called lamb's lettuce because its dark green leaves resemble a lamb's tongue. The French call it *mâche*. It is easy to grow in the garden and will withstand the frost. Well worth looking out for when it is in season.

Endive
With its slightly bitter flavor, this makes an interesting addition to winter salads. Choose firm, tightly packed cones with yellow leaf tips. Avoid any with damaged leaves or leaf tips that are turning green as they will be rather too bitter. Red endive is also available. This looks particularly attractive if sliced on the diagonal.

Iceberg lettuce
This lettuce has pale green, densely packed leaves. It may appear expensive, but is extremely good value when compared with other lettuces by weight. It has a fresh crisp texture, and will keep well in the refrigerator, wrapped in a plastic bag

Oak leaf
This red-tinged, delicately flavored lettuce is good when mixed with other leaves.

Purslane
This has fleshy stalks and rosettes of succulent green leaves, which have a sharp, clean flavor. It is an excellent addition to green salads, and is widely used in France, the Middle East and Arab countries.

Radiccio

This is a variety of endive originating in Italy. It looks rather like a small tightly packed red lettuce, and is widely available. It is quite expensive, but comparatively few leaves are needed, as it has quite a bitter flavor. The leaves are a deep purple with a white contrasting rib, and add interest to any green salad.

Romaine

This is a superb crisp variety, used especially in Caesar salad. It has long, narrow, bright green leaves.

Watercress

This has a fresh, peppery taste that is an asset in many salads. It is available throughout the year, though it is less good when flowering, or early in the season when the leaves are very small.

Preparation of salad greens

Whichever salad greens you choose, they should be firm and crisp with no sign of browning or wilting. Their preparation for the salad should be undertaken with care, remembering that most salad greens bruise very easily.

To prepare salad greens, pull off and discard all damaged outer leaves, and wash the remaining leaves in cold salted water, which will remove any insects.

Dry the greens thoroughly, as any water left on the leaves will dilute the dressing. This can be done either by patting the leaves dry with paper towels, spinning them in a salad spinner, or by placing them in a clean dish cloth, gathering up the loose ends and swinging the dish cloth around vigorously. This is best done outside, as some of the water will leak through the cloth.

If the salad greens are not required immediately, they can be stored in a plastic bag in the salad drawer of a refrigerator.

Dressing the salad too early will cause the salad greens to wilt and go soft, which spoils the fresh, crunchy texture. Ideally, salad greens should be torn into manageable-sized pieces, and tossed with the dressing in a large bowl just before serving.

NUTS

In addition to color and flavor, salads need texture, which can be achieved by combining crunchy ingredients with softer fruits and vegetables, and using starchy pasta, potatoes and lentils to contrast with fresher salad ingredients such as bell peppers, celery, apples, salad greens and so on. Nuts are a particularly useful ingredient for adding texture to a salad, as they contribute a pleasant crunchiness as well as flavor. They also add to the nutritional content of a salad, as they are rich in certain vitamins and essential oils.

Many nuts taste even better if they are browned before use, and I have suggest doing this in several recipes. This applies in particular to almonds, hazelnuts, pine nuts and peanuts. To brown nuts, put them on a cookie sheet and place in a hot oven for 5–10 minutes until golden brown. Pine nuts may also be browned by placing them in a dry heavy-bottomed skillet and shaking over a high heat until golden brown.

Apple & Cider Vinegar Dressing

2 tbsp sunflower oil
2 tbsp concentrated apple juice
2 tbsp cider vinegar
1 tbsp Meaux mustard
1 garlic clove, crushed
salt and pepper

Put all the ingredients together in a screw-top jar, and shake vigorously.

Green Herb Dressing

A pretty, pale green dressing with a fresh spring-like flavor, ideal with cauliflower, broccoli or fava beans.

1/4 cup fresh parsley
1/4 cup fresh mint
1/4 cup fresh chives
1 garlic clove, crushed
2/3 cup natural yogurt
salt and pepper

Remove the stalks from the parsley and mint, and put the leaves in a blender or food processor with the garlic and yogurt. Add seasoning to taste. Blend until smooth, then store in refrigerator until needed.

INDEX